CONTENTS

All words in **bold** can be found in the glossary on page 31

WHAT IS FREERUNNING?

A freerunner clears a low wall with a stunning side flip.

Freerunning is a spectacular activity where runners use an incredible mixture of athletic skill and gymnastics to move through an urban obstacle course. The aim is to move as easily and smoothly as possible. It is about finding your own way to move through the space with absolute freedom – that is why it is called freerunning.

A CONCRETE PLAYGROUND

Freerunners usually train in cities and towns which they use as concrete playgrounds. Runners climb, swing, jump, **vault** and roll to tackle obstacles, such as stairs, walls and buildings. They try to progress smoothly from one movement to the next without losing **momentum**.

How to be a...
FREERUNNING
CHAMPION

James Nixon

W

FRANKLIN WATTS
LONDON • SYDNEY

First published in 2015 by
Franklin Watts
338 Euston Road
London NW1 3BH

Franklin Watts Australia
Level 17/207 Kent Street
Sydney NSW 2000

© 2015 Franklin Watts

ISBN 978 1 4451 3626 4
Library eBook ISBN 978 1 4451 3628 8
Dewey classification number: 796.9

In preparation of this book, all due care has been exercised with regard to the advice, activities and techniques depicted. The publishers regret that they can accept no liability for any loss or injury sustained. When learning a new activity, it is important to get expert tuition and to follow a manufacturer's instructions.

A CIP catalogue record for this publication is available from the British Library.

Planning and production by Discovery Books Limited
Managing Editor: Paul Humphrey
Editor: James Nixon
Design: sprout.uk.com
Picture research: James Nixon

Printed in China

Franklin Watts is a division of Hachette Children's Books, an Hachette UK Company.
www.hachette.co.uk

Photo acknowledgements: Cover photo: (Alamy: Extreme Sports Photo)
Alamy: pp. 5 (ZUMA Press, Inc), 15 bottom (Roger Bamber), 16 (Ira Berger), 18 (Paul Carstairs), 19 top (Top Photo Corporation), 22 top (Buzz Pictures), 22 bottom (GoodSportHD.com), 24 top (Stuart Holt), 26 (Barry Lewis), 27 top (ZUMA Press, Inc). Getty Images: pp. 11 top (DMITRY KOSTYUKOV/AFP), 11 bottom (Samo Vidic), 19 bottom (Samo Vidic), 20 top (Darryl Leniuk), 23 top (Alex Todd/Barcroft Media), 23 bottom (Vladimir Rys Photography), 27 bottom (Predrag Vuckovic), 28 (Mark Wieland), 29 (Samo Vidic). Shutterstock: pp. 4 (Brooke Whatnall), 6 (Sergey Goruppa), 7 top (John Lumb), 8 (Val Thoermer), 9 top (Ammentorp Photography), 10 (Ammentorp Photography), 12 (Rommel Canlas), 13 bottom (Olexa), 14 (Olexa), 15 top (Brooke Whatnall), 17 top (Arturo Limon), 17 middle and bottom (Rommel Canlas), 20 bottom (Ammentorp Photography), 21 (George Muresan), 24 bottom (Velychko), 25 top (Paul Cowan). Wikimedia: pp. 7 bottom (Patrick Dep), 9 bottom (Jon Lucas), 13 top (Eleazar Castillo), 25 bottom (Hepatgon).

Every attempt has been made to clear copyright. Should there be any inadvertent omission please apply to the publisher for rectification.

THE HISTORY BIT

In the 1980s, in the streets of Paris, a group of young men developed the skills that freerunners now use. They called their form of running 'parkour' which comes from the French word *parcours* which means 'route' or 'course'.

The popularity of parkour began to increase in the late 1990s, when the group sent videos of their eye-catching movements to a French TV programme. With the word out, the interest in parkour began to spread around the globe. In the 2000s it was renamed freerunning and its techniques started to be seen in films, adverts and video games.

WANT TO RUN?

Freerunning is more often an art form than a sport. However, parkour is starting to become a recognised sport, with competitions and events held across the world. Freerunners need strength, stamina, creativity, nerves of steel and a great sense of balance. This book will introduce you to the main techniques used in freerunning. But remember, freerunning is dangerous. Never attempt it without proper training or supervision.

TOP DOG

Sebastien Foucan, born in 1974 in Paris, France, was one of the founders of parkour and was responsible for adding more and more tricks to the basic moves of parkour. In 2003, Foucan became famous in the UK when he starred in a documentary called *Jump London*, in which he ran across historic London buildings. He has also appeared in many movies including the James Bond film *Casino Royale*.

Freerunning legend Sebastien Foucan shows off his skills in *Casino Royale*.

GETTING STARTED

The best thing about freerunning is that you don't need any special equipment or clothing. You don't have to pay to use any facilities either. It is just you and your surroundings.

GEAR GUIDE

The only piece of kit that is essential to spend money on is a good pair of running shoes. An ideal pair of trainers will be lightweight but comfortable, with enough cushioning to support your feet as you land. The soles should also offer you plenty of grip. Some sport shoes manufacturers have started to design shoes especially for freerunners.

Tracksuit bottoms or shorts with a T-shirt or vest top are the usual outfit of choice. Clothes must be light and loose enough for freerunners to perform their moves. Some runners choose to wear thin, athletic gloves to protect their hands. However, most runners prefer the feeling of handling obstacles with their bare hands.

A good pair of trainers and some loose sportswear are the only equipment a freerunner needs.

WHERE TO RUN?

You can practise freerunning in any public space of your choice. It may be a park, playground or city street. Freerunning might even become a cheap form of transport for you. You will soon start to see the structures around you in a whole new light. In your mind, walls, rails and buildings will become pathways and opportunities for jumps.

In freerunning it is important to respect people and places. Never run across private property. This is called trespassing and is illegal. Freerunners also aim to leave no trace of their activity. They do not run in places where they may cause damage, and avoid running in crowded areas where they may frighten or hurt pedestrians.

Only practise freerunning on obstacles that you are sure you won't damage.

Try to find a freerunning group to help you learn the basic moves of parkour.

WARNING!

Freerunning is a highly dangerous activity if you attempt something beyond your limits. Start by just learning the basic moves. It is best to learn the sport as part of a freerunning group. The members of a group may have an experienced coach to teach you and will look out for your safety. A group will also give you encouragement and pass on their skills to you.

TRAIN YOUR BODY

Freerunning is an excellent way to stay fit and healthy. It works out your whole body and almost every move tests all of your major muscle groups. However, your body is your only tool, so make sure you look after it.

STRONGER...

As well as working out all your muscles, freerunning strengthens the connecting parts of your body – **tendons** and **ligaments**. Tendons connect muscle to bone while ligaments connect bone to bone.

It is very important to progress slowly. Do not rush into powerful movements or big jumps. Tendons and ligaments take longer than muscles to strengthen. If you attempt too much too soon you can rip or tear these delicate tissues. Try to gradually add speed and harder skills, improving your strength and **flexibility** as you go.

Before you attempt any hard parkour skills you need to train to build up your strength, power and fitness.

...AND STRONGER

The human body was not designed for bouncing and dropping on to hard concrete. Without proper training you are bound to damage yourself. Train as often as possible, starting with all types of running (jogging and sprinting) and basic jumps and landings. This will toughen up your tendons and ligaments so that you are ready for the demands of parkour.

A HEALTHY BODY AND MIND

To be a freerunner you must be extremely fit and healthy. Being healthy doesn't just mean training regularly. It is a whole way of life. It means finding a good balance between exercising, resting and eating well. It is also important to enjoy yourself. If you don't enjoy your training you won't stick to it long enough to gain from it.

Freerunning also requires a strong mind. Fear will cause you to tense up and make mistakes. You need to be confident enough to try moves at the same time as being sensible about what you can achieve. The aim is to become comfortable with the basics and progress from there.

Running, jumping and climbing are the three main types of movement that need to be trained for in parkour.

Top freerunner Daniel Ilabaca is good enough to carry out dangerous moves like this balance on a high wall.

TOP DOG

Born in England in 1988, Daniel Ilabaca is one of the world's leading freerunners. He is known for his original moves and tricks that very few runners have ever attempted. But it took years of training for Ilabaca to become this good. In 2007 he helped to found the World Freerunning and Parkour Federation, which is 'dedicated to the safe and respectful advancement of the parkour movement throughout the world'. Ilabaca is one of the most watched freerunners in the world with over 30 million YouTube views!

READY TO RUN

Before you begin any sort of freerunning, you need to warm up your body. Warming up will improve your flexibility and greatly reduce the chance of you getting injured.

WARM-UP

You need to develop a warm-up routine that covers all of the muscles and **joints**. Start with some light exercise such as a slow jog to get the blood flowing and your body temperature raised.

You then should start to exercise the joints and muscles you are going to use in your freerunning session. It might sound strange, but a good way to do this is to run around on all fours like an animal, moving and stretching your limbs in all directions. You can add rolls to your movements, too.

WARM DOWN

Note that after every freerunning session you should have a warm-down period as well. Bring your heart rate down gradually with some slow running or walking. Stretching is important to ease the tension out of your muscles. This will stop them aching afterwards. And remember to drink lots of water to replace the fluids you have lost.

Stretching is a vital part of warming up and warming down.

AREA CHECK

Most of your training should be done near ground level where you can develop your skills safely. Before you freerun you must check around your training area to see that it is safe to use. Clear away any obstructions or dangers that lie near your path. Make sure the obstacles you are using are solid and unbroken.

FIRST STEPS

There are some freerunning moves you must get right from the very start. None is more important than knowing how to land. Dropping from any height sends a shock through your body, so you need to learn how to **absorb** that shock.

As you land, relax and don't lock your legs as you hit the ground. You will find it easier to do this if you don't hold your breath. Land on the **balls** of your feet as quietly and softly as possible, **compressing** your legs and body to spread the shock through many of your muscles. Practise this technique over and over again.

By landing on the balls of your feet you will find it easier to balance.

TOP DOG

Luci Romberg (left) from the USA is one the most famous female freerunners. Romberg is also a professional stuntwoman, who has starred in blockbuster films such as *Indiana Jones and the Kingdom of the Crystal Skull*. Competing against men in freerunning competitions around the world, she became the first woman to reach the finals of the famous Red Bull Art Of Motion in 2010. Romberg says 'Freerunning is scary, it's hard, it takes a lot of courage and hitting the concrete, but it's my life and I love it'.

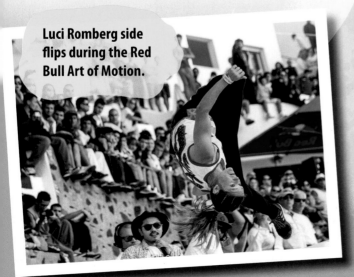

Luci Romberg side flips during the Red Bull Art of Motion.

11

LANDING AND ROLLING

Knowing how to fall without slamming hard into the ground is a key skill for freerunners. Depending on the movement you are performing there are different ways to land.

STRAIGHT LANDING

Start by learning a basic landing on both legs together from a low wall. As you jump from an obstacle, focus on your landing area so that you can time your landing. While dropping, keep your legs slightly bent and the front part of the foot angled towards the ground so that you are ready to land.

Land with the balls of the feet first and allow your legs to bend further to absorb the shock. Make sure your body and joints land in a straight line. If it helps, you can drop forward on to your hands. Then push off with your hands to start running immediately.

STEEP DROPS

Be warned that only after years of training are freerunners able to drop from seriously high levels. Without the correct preparation and training you can cause long-term damage to your body. Always work within your limits.

The top freerunners know how to fall with skill. As they drop through the air, they lean forward slightly and prepare their muscles for landing. They usually either roll out of a landing or drop into a sprinter's crouch before pushing off to run.

Learning how to land from any sort of drop is one of the first skills you should practise.

TOP DOG

David Belle (right) was one of the leading pioneers of parkour in France in the 1980s. He was inspired by his father Raymond, who was a firefighter. Raymond trained his son in gymnastics and running from a young age. David developed parkour because he wanted to find something that could be used by people in emergency situations. For him it was all about getting somewhere as fast as you can, despite the obstacles.

ROLLS

A roll is a great way to absorb the shock of an impact and keep your momentum going. It also allows you to try jumps from greater heights. The basic rolling technique in parkour uses the fleshy parts of your body rather than bony parts such as the spine and head. You can practise the basic roll from a walk, run or small drop to see how it feels.

1 Turn your body at a 45-degree angle with your shoulder and leg forward.

2 Bend your legs to land, but touch down with your hands and roll forward over your front shoulder.

3 Keep your head to the side with your chin and legs tucked in.

4 Roll through the side of your lower body on to your leg and up on to your toes.

5 Push your hands into the ground to come out of the roll back up into the running position.

A roll must begin as soon as you make contact with the ground.

13

JUMPING

Jumping is another key move that a freerunner must master early on. Often, some kind of jump is the only way to clear a gap or obstacle.

Raising your knees as you jump will give you more distance and a softer landing.

STANDING JUMPS

A standing jump has no run-up. With a swing of the arms, just push off and stretch into the jump with your whole body. You need strong stomach muscles as well as powerful legs for this. Again the best way to train for jumping is to practise – a lot!

To take off from a standing jump you need to lean into the jump and push as hard as you can with your legs. For maximum distance, raise your knees in the air and extend your feet towards your landing area. As always, aim to land softly and in control.

RUNNING JUMPS

On a running jump you can leap much further but the downside is that the landings become harder. Build up to long running jumps by practising standing jumps and shorter jumps.

The run-up to your jump should be on the balls of your feet and fast, but controlled so that every stride you make is equal to the last. Try to take off at a 45-degree angle as this will give you the most distance. You will probably have a favourite leg to take off from, but practise on both sides equally.

A running jump will help you to clear large gaps.

PRECISION

Sometimes freerunners need to land their jump on a small area, such as a narrow wall. This takes what is called **precision** jumping. Practise this at ground level before moving to greater heights.

Swing your arms to power your precision jump and land with your arms out in front of you to help you balance in the landing zone.

Jumping between walls of different angles and heights takes superb balance. You may have to turn your body sideways as you jump and **stagger** your landing so that you land on one foot before the other. For precision, try jumping higher, as coming down on to an obstacle will give you a better chance of balancing and controlling your landing.

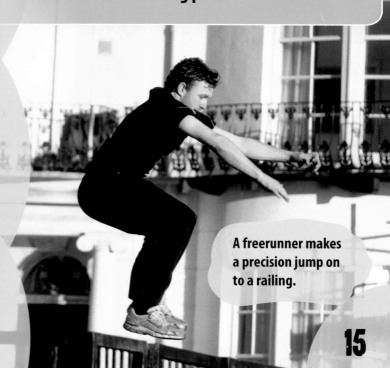

A freerunner makes a precision jump on to a railing.

MOUNTS AND VAULTS

In freerunning you have to move fluidly between different levels as you tackle obstacles such as walls and rails. A mount is when you pop up on to a low wall. A vault is when you place your hands on a low obstacle as you jump it.

USING MOUNTS

A mount lets you get up on to an obstacle in one smooth movement. From this new level you are now ready to move in the next direction. To pop up on to a wall below chest height, place your hands on the wall and jump up to land your feet between your hands.

The key to a good mount is to be quick and soft. Run up to the obstacle and land one foot slightly in front of the other if you can, so that you can continue to run in your next direction without stopping.

CORKSCREW

A 'corkscrew pop-up' lets you change the direction you are travelling in. Place your palms down on the obstacle with one set of fingers pointed back towards you. Spin around these fingers as you jump up to face the opposite way.

RAIL MOUNT

A rail mount needs precision and balance as the landing area is thin. You need to be able to crouch on a thin rail or bar without falling forwards or backwards. It's worth practising rail mounts over and over again to improve your balancing skills.

Practising rail mounts will help you to improve your balance.

VAULTING

Low walls, handrails and tables are common obstacles that you can vault over in one movement. The aim is to jump forwards into the vault, not upwards, so that you don't slow down. So, with good speed, don't take off too close to the obstacle.

Place your hands on top of the obstacle as you pass over it. Make sure you have good grip with your hands so that you can vault over in perfect control. Land on one foot the other side so that you can continue running.

You can vault over a park bench if it is fixed solidly to the ground.

Be light on an obstacle as you vault it, and try to keep your momentum going forwards.

STEP VAULT

A step vault (left) is the safest way to clear an obstacle below chest height. Take off on one leg and bring your other leg up to step on to the obstacle at the same time as placing your hand on it. Your trailing leg then comes up between your body and the top of the obstacle to land on the other side.

TURN VAULT

On a turn vault, you can stop and hang on to the other side of an obstacle for a second. This is useful if you are not sure of the drop below you. Place both hands on the obstacle with one hand pointing backwards, and turn in mid-air around the hand. This hand stays on the obstacle while the other is lifted off as you turn. As you reach the other side, grip the obstacle again with your loose hand.

On a turn vault you can pause on the other side of the obstacle to check out your next move.

A BALANCING ACT

The ability to balance is a key part of freerunning.
As well as helping you to vault and precision jump,
it is vital for moving swiftly on narrow surfaces.

Use your arms to help keep your balance on thin walls.

GET STEADY

If you feel a bit wobbly when you start freerunning – don't worry. Balance is a skill that can be developed. Every training session should include some balance work. By using the muscles you need to balance yourself over and over again you will feel much steadier.

A simple exercise for balance is the slow crouch. With your legs shoulder-width apart stand up on the balls of your feet and crouch down until your buttocks touch your heels. Hold this for five seconds and then stand up slowly, still on the balls of your feet. When you are out walking always look for a kerb or low rail to practise your balance on.

RAIL WALKING

The top freerunners can move quickly along thin and rounded railings that have little grip. Before you attempt rails like this, practise on surfaces of different thicknesses and materials. Learn to walk with your feet in line with the rail and try to sway as little as possible.

THE CAT BALANCE

The 'cat balance' is a technique used by freerunners to move along narrow walls and rails. The runner scampers along the obstacle like a cat. On all fours, stretch out on the object with your weight on all of your limbs equally. To keep moving forwards, move your rear arm ahead of your front arm and your rear leg ahead of your front leg. Keep your hips low and try to move as swiftly as possible without stopping.

The cat balance is a great way to improve strength in your whole body.

Jesse La Flair

RECORD BREAKERS

Professional freerunner Jesse La Flair from the USA has become a household name in parkour and an Internet sensation. Like many freerunners, La Flair started posting videos of his training and adventures on YouTube. Now he is the most **subscribed** freerunner in the world with over 230,000 YouTube followers. He has helped to inspire many young freerunners with his video **tutorials**.

WALL RUNS

Freerunners can overcome obstacles that you would never think of attempting. If a wall is too high to vault or jump over, they can run up it!

HOW TO DO IT

Wall runs are moves that most freerunners love to learn. They can be used to pass a wall over twice your own height! A wall run requires lots of power in the legs. You also need good **coordination**, so that you can reach up to grab the top of the wall at the right time. Here is how it's done.

Running up walls is not just for superheroes!

1 Run up to the wall head-on with good pace.

2 Just before the wall, start to angle your body back and look up at the wall. Your last couple of steps need to be powerful.

3 Jump with your lead foot on to the surface of the wall at waist height and push upwards.

4 As you push off, use your arms to drive your body up and stretch to grab the top of the wall with both hands.

5 You now need strength in your shoulders and arms to pull yourself up on to the top of the wall (right).

WALLS AS FLOORS

As a freerunner you soon start to see walls as vertical floors. You can step on to a wall and push off it to land elsewhere. This kind of move is called a tic-tac. In fact, you can tic-tac off pretty much any object as long as it is solid enough. A tic-tac has many uses. It can be used to help you vault over a high railing for example.

HOW TO TIC-TAC

Use your leg nearest the wall to tic-tac, but don't get too close to the wall so that your leg bunches up. Your aim is to bounce off the surface quickly. Strike the wall with the ball of your foot, with the toes pointing upwards. Turn your body quickly to face the way you want to go, and push upwards off the wall to give yourself extra height.

To get even more height on a tic-tac, you can take more than one step on the wall. Remember to lean away from the wall as you step on it. If you are too upright you will slip downwards.

As you push off a wall during a tic-tac, aim to push upwards as well as away from the wall.

RECORD BREAKERS

In 2012, German parkour athlete Amadei Weiland set the record for the longest wall run ever. He ran up a wall that measured 3.49 metres high!

LEAPING AND SWINGING

The leaps and swings made by freerunners can look similar to the way monkeys swing though the trees. Expert freerunners can make giant leaps to cross gaps that look impossible.

CAT LEAPS

An arm jump, known as a 'cat leap', is one way of jumping across a gap if you can't reach the other side to land on your feet. Instead you can catch the ledge of the obstacle opposite and climb up it.

A running arm jump is tricky because you will land up against the face of the obstacle with some force. Try to make the impact softer by extending your arms and legs forward as you prepare to land. Then land both legs and arms at the same time, bending them to absorb the shock. Use the bounce back off the wall to help pull yourself up.

CRANE JUMPS

If you can jump far enough to land one of your feet on top of an obstacle, you can do the 'crane jump'. While in the air, lift up your front knee to make sure your foot reaches the top. As you land, hang your rear leg beneath you up against the obstacle to help you balance, and push off straight away without stopping.

Two freerunners put their arms out as they attempt to make a cat leap.

On a crane jump land on your lead foot with the other leg beneath you.

Freerunners can swing on a bar a few times to build up momentum.

SWING TIME

By grabbing and swinging off horizontal rails, freerunners can leap with strength and grace. The key to a good swing is using your whole body to create power. Use your lower legs to swing your body and, when your hips are high and out in front of you, let go of the bar. At the same time pull with your arms for extra power.

If you are jumping to another bar make sure you catch it with a good grip. However, stay relaxed and don't lock your arms up as you make the catch.

TOP DOG

Born in 1992, Pasha Petkuns (left) from Latvia, nicknamed 'The Boss', is currently one of the top freerunners in the world. He stands out because of his creative swinging moves on the bars and the bounciness of his movements. Petkuns was victorious in the Red Bull Art of Motion in 2011 and 2012, impressing the judges with his style and risk-taking.

23

ACROBATICS

Some freerunners choose to add incredible and eye-catching acrobatics to the basic movements of parkour. These stunts can be used to dazzle the judges and crowds in competitions.

The webster somersault is one of the most spectacular moves in freerunning.

HEAD OVER HEELS

For the top freerunners, a 'webster' somersault is a stunning way to get down a set of stairs or a slope. The runner takes off from one foot and kicks the other leg up behind them to fly head over heels. Then they land on the trailing leg and carry on running.

PALM SPINS

The wall spin is a neat-looking move. The runner jumps up towards a wall, places their palms on it, and then flips over their bottom hand to land back down on the ground. It is easiest to first learn this move by trying it with one palm on the wall and the other on the ground.

The wall spin is one of many freerunning moves that involve spinning on the palm of your hands.

If you ever want to try acrobatics such as this side flip you should find a qualified gymnastics instructor.

FLIPS

The side flip is an impressive way of clearing a low object without touching it. It is basically a sideways somersault. The runner runs hard and fast before taking off into the air side-on. They stretch the arms forward and tuck their knees in to rotate throughout the air before landing.

On 'back tucks' freerunners throw themselves backwards off a low wall or other obstacle. After flipping over a full turn, they land upright on their feet. Moves like these are for experts only and require years of freerunning training.

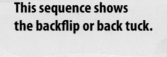

This sequence shows the backflip or back tuck.

RECORD BREAKERS

The longest ever side flip was achieved by Jordan Davis in Missouri, USA, in 2012. He flipped a whopping distance of 4.65 metres!

In 2010 Matthew Kaye from the UK set a record of 17 front somersaults in just one minute!

ON LOCATION

You can practise freerunning almost anywhere but some hotspots in the world have become famous for their freerunning opportunities.

A WORLD SPORT

Lisses is the town in France where the first freerunners invented their moves. The obstacles they used are still there today, such as the *Dame du Lac*, an artificial climbing structure in the town's park.

Since then London and many other cities have developed a freerunning culture. San Francisco and Miami in the USA have large freerunning communities. Freerunning has also become popular in cities such as Sydney, São Paulo and Beijing. The sport is now truly global.

THE WFPF

The World Freerunning Parkour Federation (WFPF) was founded in 2007 by eight of the world's most respected parkour athletes. Their aim was to bring the sport of parkour to a wider audience.

In 2010 the WFPF produced 12 episodes of *Ultimate Parkour Challenge*, which were screened on MTV weekly. Each week the freerunners were put in new environments to compete. The first episode was filmed in Long Beach, California.

A freerunner somersaults past the London Eye.

TOP DOG

Ryan Doyle (right), born in 1984 in Liverpool, UK, was one of the founding athletes of the WFPF. Doyle was also the winner of the first ever Red Bull Art of Motion held in Vienna, Austria, in 2007. As a teenager Doyle trained in **martial arts**. He discovered that by adding parkour movements to his martial arts techniques he had a special talent for freerunning.

ART OF MOTION

The best freerunners get together at least once every year for the most important event on the calendar – The Red Bull Art of Motion. It has been held in various countries including England, Kuwait and Sweden. For the last four years it has been held on the island of Santorini in Greece.

In 2014 a total of 18 freerunners took on the Santorini course one by one to show off their own unique tricks. In front of 1,500 spectators they had to leap across whitewashed roofs, domes and terraces in a timed run of 90 seconds. Local hero Dimitris Kyrsanidis (left) took a shock win as his flow and creativity earned him an almost perfect score of 494 out of 500 from the judges, pushing previous champion Pasha Petkuns into second place.

STORY OF A CHAMPION

CORY DEMEYERS

In Santorini in 2013, Cory DeMeyers became the first person from the USA to win the Red Bull Art of Motion. Here is his story.

A MARTIAL ARTIST

Cory DeMeyers grew up in a small town in Michigan, USA. At the age of 5 he started training in a traditional martial art called Tang Soo Do. For years he trained, travelled and competed all over the world, becoming a five-time Tang Soo Do world champion by the time he was 18!

DeMeyers moved to southern California to teach martial arts at a karate school and it was there in 2010 that he was introduced to the sport of freerunning. After his first training session, DeMeyers was hooked. There and then he decided freerunning was what he wanted to do in his life.

FAST TRAINING

For the first year of his freerunning career, DeMeyers trained five or six hours almost every day. He was able to learn much faster than the friends he was training with because of his martial arts background. Amazingly, within that first year, he was invited to compete in the sport's biggest event – the Red Bull Art of Motion.

Cory DeMeyers poses with the winner's trophy at the 2013 Red Bull Art of Motion.

Cory DeMeyers in action at the Red Bull Art of Motion in Santorini.

REACHING THE TOP

Ten days before his first Art of Motion Demeyers broke his foot, but decided he had to compete anyway for fear of never being invited back! By 2012 he had joined the team Tempest Freerunning and realised his dream of becoming a professional athlete.

In his winning performance in the 2013 Art of Motion DeMeyers had to master the 200-metre long course inside a two-minute time limit. His spectacular and fluid movements saw him given a score of 449 points, enough to take the title by just two points from runner-up Alexander Baiturin from Russia.

STUNTMAN

DeMeyers is not only a star in the world of sports. He is also a spectacular stuntman who has appeared in many adverts, televison shows and blockbuster films. The movies he has performed stunts in include *300: Rise of an Empire* and *Star Trek: Into Darkness*. In the 2015 action film *The Last Witch Hunter* he acted as a stunt double for actor Elijah Wood.

A PASSION

DeMeyer's passion is to create new styles of movement that have never been seen before. In doing this he hopes to inspire others to follow in his footsteps. His tip is to move in a way that makes you happy and discover your own style.

FIND OUT MORE

BOOKS

The Parkour & Freerunning Handbook, *Dan Edwardes, (Virgin Books 2009)*

The Ultimate Parkour & Freerunning Book, *Ilona Gerling, Axel Pach and Jan Whitfield, (Meyer & Meyer Sport 2013)*

Free Running: A Beginner's Guide on Training in Parkour and Free Running, *Zach Rucker, (CreateSpace Independent Publishing Platform 2014)*

Radar: Free Running, *Paul Mason and Sarah Eason, (Wayland 2011)*

Adrenalin Rush: Free Running, *Jackson Teller, (Franklin Watts 2013)*

WEBSITES

www.wikihow.com/Category:Parkour
A series of 'How to…' guides for freerunners

www.wfpf.com
Home of the World Freerunning Parkour Federation with parkour news from around the world

www.parkouruk.org/joinin
Find a freerunning group to join

www.parkourtrain.net/topics/physical-conditioning
Learn how to train your body for freerunning

www.apexmovement.com/blog/how-to-start-parkour-a-beginners-guide
A beginner's guide to parkour

http://parkourpedia.com/technique
Learn how to master the basic parkour skills

www.listofmoves.co.uk/list-of-free-running-moves
Watch the videos of these acrobatic freerunning tricks

Website disclaimer: Note to parents and teachers: Every effort has been made by the Publishers to ensure that these websites are suitable for children, that they are of the highest educational value, and that they contain no inappropriate or offensive material. However, because of the nature of the Internet, it is impossible to guarantee that the contents of these sites will not be altered. We strongly advise that Internet access is supervised by a responsible adult.

GLOSSARY

absorb reduce the affect of an impact such as landing on hard ground

balls the part of the sole of your foot just behind the toes

compressing squeezing into a smaller space

coordination the ability to move different parts of the body at the same time

flexibility the ability to bend easily without injuring yourself

joints parts of the body where two bones are fitted together

ligament tough but flexible tissue which connects two bones together

martial arts sports or skills which originated as forms of self-defence or attack, such as judo or karate

momentum the power or force gained by moving or progressing

pioneer a person who is first to develop a new idea or set of techniques

precision the skill of being accurate

Red Bull Art of Motion a competition held at least once every year contested by the best freerunners in the world

stagger place your feet so that they are not in line with each other

subscribed signed up to view or receive something over a period of time

tendon a cord of strong tissue attaching muscle to a bone

tutorial a lesson to help you learn something

vault leap or spring over an obstacle, while supporting yourself with your hands

INDEX